TRADITIONAL NOW

TRADITIONAL NOW

INTERIORS BY DAVID KLEINBERG

DAVID KLEINBERG *with* CHESIE BREEN

Foreword *by* Albert Hadley

THE MONACELLI PRESS

Copyright © 2011 by The Monacelli Press, a division of Random House, Inc.

All rights reserved. Published in the United States by The Monacelli Press, a division of Random House, Inc., New York

The Monacelli Press and the M design are registered trademarks of Random House, Inc.

LIBRARY OF CONGRESS CATALOGING-IN-PUBLICATION DATA

Kleinberg, David.
Traditional now : interiors by David Kleinberg / David Kleinberg with Chesie Breen ; foreword by Albert Hadley. — 1st ed.
p.   cm.
ISBN 978-1-58093-322-3
1. Kleinberg, David—Themes, motives.
2. Interior decoration—United States—History—20th century. 3. Interior decoration—United States—History—21st century. I. Breen, Chesie. II. Title. III. Title: Interiors by David Kleinberg.
NK2004.3.K59A4   2011
747.092—dc22   2011011091

Printed in China

www.monacellipress.com

10 9 8 7 6 5 4 3 2 1
First edition

Designed by pulp, ink.

PHOTOGRAPHY CREDITS

Christopher Baker: 78–79, 80–81

Fernando Bengochea: 218, 224, 225

Dale Curtis: 198–99, 200, 203, 204–5

Pieter Estersohn: 24–25, 26, 28–29, 30, 31, 32–33, 34, 36–37, 38–39, 40–41, 42–43, 46–47, 48–49, 50, 52, 55, 56, 57, 59, 106–7, 108, 110–11, 112, 113, 114–15, 116, 117, 118–19, 120, 122–23, 124, 125, 126–27, 128–29, 130–31, 132–33, 134, 135, 148–49, 150, 152–53, 154–55, 156, 157, 158–59, 160–61, 162–63, 164, 167, 168–69, 170–71, 172–73, 174, 175, 176–77, 178, 179,180–81, 182–83, 184–85, 186, 188–89, 190–91, 192, 193, 195, 196–97, 216–17, 230, 231, 232–33, 234, 235, 236, 237

Tria Giovan: 142, 146–47

Ken Hayden: 220, 221

Thomas Loof: 60–61, 62, 64–65, 66, 68, 69, 70–71

Peter Murdock: 72–73, 74, 76, 77, 81, 82, 83, 136–37, 138, 140–41, 142–43, 144–45

Eric Piasecki: 84–85, 86, 89, 90, 91, 92–93

Sargeant Architectural Photography: 206–7, 208, 210–11, 212, 213, 214–15

Durston Saylor: 94–95, 96, 98–99, 100, 101, 102, 103, 104, 105

Francesca Sorrenti: 222, 223

William Waldron: 40, 44, 45, 226, 227, 228, 229

CONTENTS

FOREWORD

Albert Hadley

Traditional Now is a provocative title for this volume of distinguished work that David Kleinberg has produced. The title somehow suggests to me that perhaps the designer has employed his talents and his strong cultivated taste to present an aesthetic handed down by, or deferring to, tradition. But that is far from true!

This is a very beautiful and handsome book that reveals a cogent philosophy and is accompanied by photographs of distinguished twentieth- and twenty-first-century interiors. The text that accompanies each project—each photograph—is Kleinberg's own and is of paramount interest for many reasons, but especially because it shows his imagination, positive spirit, and humor. Each interior is notable partly because the author obviously has no hesitation in carefully selecting furnishings, objects, and artwork from past eras to complement and support a constant modern—a "now" point of view.

It must be noted here that David Kleinberg's creativity is more than just obvious "decorating"; it is based on an architectural refinement that embraces all details and finishes, many of which are clearly viewed in the images presented in this book.

INTRODUCTION

It's common for interior decorators to talk about how their interest in design can be traced to the houses they grew up in. But I grew up in a rather unremarkable house on the North Shore of Long Island, where becoming a decorator was not a typical aspiration for the boys of my generation. I was supposed to become a doctor or lawyer. My appreciation for houses developed as a result of a friendship with my across-the-fence neighbor whose father was an established builder. I was intrigued by his collection of trade magazines and spent hours tracing and analyzing the houses showcased. My interest in architecture and interior design was as much of a surprise to me as it was to my family. When I left for Trinity College in Connecticut for undergraduate studies in 1972, my plan was to set a course for architecture school.

The more I learned, the more I became fixated on beautiful houses and high-end residential design. I became convinced that architecture school would lead to corporate, institutional work, and becoming a "gentleman architect" wasn't an option. I was lucky to have a friend whose family home was being decorated by the formidable Denning & Fourcade; her mother offered to make an introduction, and I was hired to work for the firm during summers and after college.

Working for Robert Denning and Vincent Fourcade, who lived as well as their well-heeled clients, was a head-spinning experience. At the top of their field, they had a client list that included Mrs. Ogden Phipps, Jacqueline Kennedy Onassis, Françoise de la Renta, and Diane von Furstenberg. Vincent Fourcade's own townhouse gave new meaning to Belle Epoque. My childhood home had Herman Miller and Knoll, which was considered

pretty up-market but was nothing compared to all of the Charles X and Louis Philippe that surrounded these men. There were blue-and-white Chinese export vases on brackets reaching all the way to the ceiling and Rigaud candles burning everywhere. It was my first exposure to the good life, and I was enthralled.

Eventually I yearned for more responsibility, and through the network of showroom managers at the Decoration & Design Building, I met the venerable Mara Palmer, who split her time between New York and Geneva. Exotic, stylish, and able to speak eleven languages, this Bulgarian force knocked me off my feet and became an important influence on my career. Her prolonged absences from the office gave me the best sort of training by placing me in charge of all manner of tasks. I started the day making coffee for the office, shopped the D&D Building, called on antiques dealers, met

with clients, culled estimates, prepared orders, arranged truckers, and ran the vacuum before I left. Mara was full of life and generous; we had a terrific working and personal relationship. After five rewarding years, there was no other place I would have worked—except one.

Parish-Hadley was considered the pinnacle of the profession, representing the most celebrated families in the country. The work epitomized the highest standards and talent in an industry that had yet to really define itself. I had been introduced to Albert Hadley in 1976 by Frederick Victoria, a well-established antiques dealer. While Albert had no position to offer me at the time, I stayed in contact with him during my tenure with Mara. When my friend Gary Hager, who worked for Parish-Hadley as junior decorator—the position I had hoped to obtain five years prior—informed me in 1981 that they were looking to hire a decorator, needless to say I leapt at the chance.

Their conference room, which was decorated as a comfortable living room in shades of beige, chocolate brown, and coral, confirmed not only my choice of interior design as lifelong career but that

Parish-Hadley was where I needed to be. At the scheduled time, Mrs. Parish entered the room followed closely by her two Pekingese. As if on cue, one squatted and I jumped for the paper towels and volunteered to wipe up the mess; to this day I'm convinced that was the reason I got the job. I went to Parish-Hadley expecting to work with Albert Hadley since my inclination toward design was aligned with his pared-down aesthetic. To my surprise, I was scooped up by Mrs. Parish and worked on every project with her for the next twelve years.

One of my great career lessons has been that your best references are your clients, and your best clients are the ones who return. During this time we would do five projects for Henryk and Barbara de Kwiatkowski. The first was Conyers Farm, a 1920s garage and chauffeur's cottage in Greenwich, Connecticut, that had been converted into an impressive country

home; it was in need of renovation and expansion. This project was a full expression of everything that Mrs. Parish loved: braided rugs, chintz, beautiful curtains, canopied beds, overstuffed upholstery, and an overriding sense of comfort.

Conyers Farm marked the first time I witnessed Mrs. Parish's innate ability to understand how a house should function and to predict how people would inhabit it. She walked the property, studied the spaces, and after listening to everything the Harvard-trained architect Alan Wanzenberg was saying, politely replied, "Listen young man—you realize you have the front door on the wrong side of the house." This stopped everyone in their tracks.

Though Mrs. Parish never put her vision on paper, she could pull a pitch-perfect furniture plan out of thin air, mesmerizing those of us who then implemented

that image. She was raised in a genteel world that had already disappeared, and her upbringing informed her decisions. She gave me a window into the sense of knowing what's called for in all aspects of decorating a home; that can't be learned in a classroom.

Following Conyers Farm, an apartment on Beekman Place, a house in Palm Beach, and a villa at Lyford Cay in the Bahamas, the de Kwiatkowskis made headlines in 1992 by saving from ruin the fabled Calumet Farm in Lexington, Kentucky. Built in the 1920s, it was the country's preeminent race horse farm—850 acres in size. We were their first phone call. But at that point Mrs. Parish's health had started to fail, so it fell to me to channel the experience I had gleaned from sitting next to this formidable woman and create a great American country house. From the outset, I strived for a sense of relaxed formality. The interiors reflect the sensibility of an

Englishman living abroad—glamorous but comfortable. Henryk wanted the interiors of all his houses to look like they had always been there, not like he had just moved in. At the same time, we wanted Calumet to convey a sense of permanence. It was the kind of house Mrs. Parish would have loved even though she wasn't able to see it completed.

When I finally did get to work with Albert Hadley it was on an apartment in the newly built Ritz-Carlton in Boston. The experience was the complete opposite but equally rewarding. Albert was always ready with his clipboard and sheets of tracing paper. He was as organized, thoughtful, and academic in his process as Mrs. Parish was intuitive. The team would sit and talk, and Albert would begin to sketch furniture plans and draw elevations. Albert taught me how to "build" a room. If Mrs. Parish was the instinctual heart of the firm, Albert was the analytical

mind. Their relationship was enviable because their different approaches were always true to the same mantra: beauty meets quality of life.

Parish-Hadley encouraged its team of decorators to develop our own clients under the firm's umbrella, which fostered independence and allowed me to develop my own aesthetic. Garrick Stephenson was an extremely respected antiques dealer with impeccable style. I would stand outside his shop window intimidated, coveting a collection that was as rare as it was varied. In 1993, this ultimate bon-vivant-antiquaire-without-a-care grew tired of his gallery and auctioned everything off at Christie's. He purchased a new apartment at One East Sixty-sixth Street, and though I was never officially hired to do the job, we realized that we had joined forces. My work on this project marked the beginning of my interest in French midcentury designers,

left and below, GARRICK STEPHENSON APARTMENT, LIVING ROOM

PARK AVENUE APARTMENT, ENTRY

PARK AVENUE APARTMENT, DINING ROOM

which would become the hallmark of my style when launching my own firm.

Twenty-one years into a career greater than I could have imagined, I began to feel it was time to start my own enterprise. When I told Albert I was leaving, he was, true to form, generous and full of encouragement. I opened the doors of David Kleinberg Design Associates in May 1997 with many of the clients I had developed at Parish-Hadley and two core team members, Kim Cruise and Brian del Toro.

I still remember the day one of my Parish-Hadley clients walked into our offices and handed me a check, officially putting me in business. That first assignment—a Park Avenue apartment—drew a lot of attention for its clean, modern aesthetic combined with sophisticated antiques. It was a symphony of whites at a time when white schemes were considered quite daring. To this day people still compliment the work.

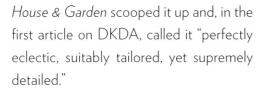

House & Garden scooped it up and, in the first article on DKDA, called it "perfectly eclectic, suitably tailored, yet supremely detailed."

Next we worked on the same client's Southampton house, a classic rose-covered cottage near the ocean. It was originally the barn of a nearby mansion, and my clients wanted to preserve its charm. The goal was to make the house functional and modern but to maintain its pastoral quality. We went to great effort to accomplish this and to create a lot of room on the inside

without making it look big on the outside. We built a new gambrel roof to balance the old and tucked a master bedroom under the dormer. The living room was expanded onto a brick terrace; a staff room became part of the kitchen. We created a two-story entrance hall with cerused oak paneling and brick floors, referencing the exterior terraces. When *Architectural Digest* described it as "a big house that looks small, a new house that looks old, a house furnished with a wild eclecticism that appears calmly uniform," I knew we had achieved what we set out to do.

My overriding principle was then, and remains now, that there is no overriding principle. I simply select things I like in a house, acquiring objects and furnishings as if done over a lifetime of collecting. This process is often referred to as my "curatorial mix." It may seem happenstance, but it is a carefully measured process. I've never been one of those decorators who want people to think there was no decorator. I don't think of myself as a cutting-edge person; I think of myself as a classical person, but a classical person in the modern world.

The Kips Bay Boys & Girls Club Decorator Show House is to decorating what opening night is to the opera: the ultimate place to exhibit talent. When I was invited to participate in 1998, it was an opportunity for me to show my work alongside the most revered names in the business and to establish my unique voice. Because I was still in the process of launching DKDA, I wanted to create a

room that clearly stated my mission: here is the new traditional.

I began by asking myself, how do I want to define traditional at the end of the twentieth century? The room brought together an unexpected mix of materials and periods; this type of assemblage, a trait that continues to characterize my body of work, gave the room an enduring sense of style. The walls were covered in burlap with hand-painted white stripes, except for the fireplace wall, which was sheathed in bronze. The curtains were of unlined burlap with wide ivory leather banding, and we used photography instead of paintings. These modern and unanticipated elements were set against a classic arrangement of traditional mahogany furniture with the strong forms I favor. With the twentieth century now well behind us, I can still say that I'd live in this room today. It's an unmistakable illustration of my notion of traditional now.

The room was published in the *New York Times*, *Traditional Home*, and *Interior Design*. This swell of favorable press on both Kips Bay and my early projects—combined with a roster of loyal clients—firmly established DKDA. In the years since then, the business has grown to include two dozen employees, an architectural department, and a sophisticated group of clients.

It's important to recognize that good design is only made better through collaboration. When I was leaving Parish-Hadley, I worried about losing my sounding board. With Mrs. Parish, I watched and absorbed, learning through osmosis. Albert was a voice of reason and inspiration; he was the mentor I turned to as I developed my ideas. But the start of DKDA saw the start of a new sounding board: my clients, my design team, and, ever stronger over the years, my own voice.

AN EQUESTRIAN EDEN

The devoted horsewoman who took this abandoned Florida citrus grove and transformed it into a working horse farm—complete with stables, paddocks, bridle trails, jump fields, and rolling pastures—is a force of nature. She was determined to make this land her Nirvana. The design of the main house was inspired by my client's visits to the Caribbean and a study of houses in Spain and the south of France. Her wish list included a barrel-tile roof incorporating three shades of terra-cotta, mahogany doors, arched doorways, creamy stucco walls, and coral stone. My challenge was to take this list and create a cohesive design statement that didn't feel like a pastiche of unrelated elements and styles.

KITCHEN

Our master plan called for anchoring the house with a central great room where the entire family could interact and engage in a variety of activities: conversation, cards and games, television, dining. An enormous limestone chimney breast based on an eighteenth-century model stretches up to a cedar-beamed cathedral ceiling. Back-to-back upholstered sofas, ideal for entertaining, center the room, which is filled with the unexpected. An eighteenth-century English walnut refectory table is flanked by rectangular benches rather than dining chairs. Offbeat, late-seventeenth-century Chinese consoles contrast with neutral, relaxed fabrics: woven cottons, linens, and raffia. In the light-soaked window bay, late-nineteenth-century oak chairs surround a sturdy game table. Though the room is grand in scale, a relaxed atmosphere prevails.

Two bedroom wings flank the central space. My bedrooms are most often about serenity, clarity, and retreat, which here steered me toward a tried-and-true color palette of watery blues and soft whites. I liked the statement the chimney breast made in the great room and employed an overmantel to similar effect in the master bedroom. In deference to my client's appreciation of British colonial style, I chose a nineteenth-century West Indian mahogany four-poster bed for the guest room, which is decorated in lemony colors. A British colonial highboy sits on top of a linen rug.

30

GUEST ROOM

The house itself is surrounded by a colonnaded breezeway. The limestone pavers inside the breezeway transform naturally into exterior coral stone porches. Steps and a lawn lead to an impressive twenty-five-by-seventy-five-foot pool, a pool house, and a fire pit. Where dying citrus trees once stood, fragrant magnolias, tulip poplars, hollies, jacarandas, sweet gums, junipers, and oleanders now bloom.

The transformation of this Florida estate is incomparable. At the outset, we stood in a field of . . . nothing, with the task of conjuring a cohesive living environment: house, paddocks, orchards, riding trails, and more. When your only confines are earth and sky, all options are possible. It is how you choose from an exhaustive wish list that is the most important ingredient.

FRENCH FLAIR
IN NEW YORK

This Park Avenue apartment has been a career touchstone. Everything in it represents the very best example of the period and style we were embracing. My clients, savvy and passionate, pushed for my strongest ideas and were willing to go the distance to see them realized. That distance included several buying trips to Paris; my clients' rigorous study of furniture periods; and a joint commitment to seeking out the very best.

LIVING ROOM

ENTRY

Our role in designing the apartment began in the architectural phase. The floor plan was reconfigured to make it feel more expansive, modern, and youthful, but in a way that maintained the integrity of the prewar building. Inspiration came from a photograph of an André Arbus entrance hall with precise proportions and an elegantly paneled door. This entry space, clean palettes, and careful selection became our spirit guides.

The entry foyer is as remarkable for what's not there as for what is. Instead of a hall table, we selected a putty-colored Jean-Michel Frank banquette and a Diego Giacometti bronze side table. Above is a 1955 Franz Kline painting. The only trace of pattern is on the floor, which is stenciled in an overscaled, abstract version of an interlocking grid.

In the living room we established a strong dialogue between eighteenth- and nineteenth-century antiques and French mid-twentieth-century furniture. Because so much French mid-twentieth-century furniture is based on eighteenth-century models, mixing the periods kept this room from becoming static and acknowledged the debt one century owes to the other. The ornate, baroque decoration of an eighteenth-century Venetian mirror is juxtaposed with the more graphic, robust form of a nineteenth-century English Regency marble mantel. A Gilbert Poillerat cocktail table, which was designed in collaboration with Serge Roche and was once in Roche's own home, and a Clement Rousseau side table further the mélange. Walls lacquered in a high-gloss pumice color maximize light and are a clean backdrop for artworks by Andy Warhol, Ellsworth Kelly, and Willem de Kooning; a Robert Motherwell oil rests on the mantel. As in the foyer, pattern is limited to the rug.

Vases made for Napoleon I flank the passage from the living room to the dining room, epitomizing our intent to marry different periods. Anchoring the dining room is a large circular table surrounded by nineteenth-century English Regency chairs upholstered in midnight blue. Brice Marden's grandly scaled *Blue Horizontal*, 1987, is the decidedly modernist star of the room. The rug is a variation on the one in the living room. Keeping the palette clean and using pattern as texture on the floors helped expand the apartment's layout and gave it the airy, loftlike quality we were striving for.

The library has a warmer palette, and varying textures enrich the tone. The curtains are woven silk, the sofa is upholstered in mohair, the rug is wool, and the walls are Ultrasuede. A Jean Dubuffet oil commands the sofa wall. The most notable element is what is left unseen: library books. The books and games are all there, but carefully concealed. In the library is an André Sornay desk my client and I acquired on one of our early trips. Months later, we visited a shop and my client, by now possessing an expert eye, immediately recognized that the proprietor's chair was the mate to her desk. Without hesitation, she bought it out from under him.

KITCHEN

44

In the kitchen, bright white surfaces, strong lines, and beautifully designed cabinetry contrast with dark, polished floors. Lightly veined marble is used for both the island and the backsplash. Three Jean Royère iron stools upholstered in embossed vinyl punctuate the counter. The adjacent family room has lighter tones, allowing the mix of furniture and art to once again take center stage. Sean Scully's *Checker Blue*, 2000, dominates one wall, and an untitled 1969 Cy Twombly hangs above the sofa. The Jacques Adnet leather chairs were another of our Paris finds.

FAMILY ROOM

The master bedroom suite offers a serene retreat above Park Avenue. It features a rare indulgence in pattern—hand-painted Gracie wallpaper in a palette of creams and taupes on a silver ground. A Eugene Printz chest of drawers with ormolu mounts and a marble top stands alongside a pair of André Arbus pear-wood chairs. The bronze-framed chairs in the dressing area are by Printz, and the benches are by Arbus.

The décor, furnishings, and art in this apartment are not about embellishment; they are about absolutes. Subtle style and nuance stem from very small strokes—a beautiful lacquer finish, an inlaid-straw treatment, ivory parchment-covered cabinet doors. Continuity and integrity come from knowing precisely what to take out and what to leave in.

AMERICANS ABROAD
RETURN

A very European-minded American couple live in this beautifully proportioned, East Side penthouse apartment. I was called in shortly after they returned from a stint in Paris. A stylish woman opened the door and explained that, though she had planned to decorate the apartment herself, she was hopelessly "stuck." Fortunately, in a glance I knew exactly what to do next.

Our tour started in the living room, which was a lovely, symmetrical room with four pairs of French doors opening to wraparound terraces. My client had painted the walls pale gray and hung leafy-green silk taffeta curtains. The curtains held court but the room was not cohesive. We needed an effective foil for the crush of green, something that could hold its own with all of the black in the room: black piano, black marble mantelpiece, black window casings. As I thought about the project, I remembered a living room Mrs. Parish had created, one that had aubergine walls and bright blue curtains. One set the other off—there was an instant sweet/sour, yin/yang moment. I decided not just to paint the walls but to glaze and varnish them to a high sheen, giving the rich eggplant color more lushness.

We employed a few more decorative manipulations in the living room. The sofa was a great shape but it was really too big for the room. So we upholstered it in wool sateen in the same shade as the walls: the shape remained important while the size faded away. The chintz-upholstered armchair is another nod to Mrs. Parish. There was a time when chintz was both overused and misused. I have never abandoned chintz, and when I do use it, however judiciously, it defines the main color palette for the room.

The dining room is a light, bright space with spots of intense color, much like a painting. The impression is especially vivid when viewed from the dark living room. We repeated the bright green curtains; chair backs upholstered in silk taffeta in sorbet colors complement them. (We left green off the list—often good decorating is knowing where to stop.) The chair seats are upholstered in bruised plum leather, which refers back to the walls of the living room.

Because our clients wanted the dining room to double as a library, we proposed a pair of tables and chandeliers. One table is used for dinner and the other for paging through books. The bookcases are lined with Il Papiro Italian marbleized paper, subtly infusing the room with rich color and dimension.

The theme of European traditions continues in the bedroom, where the bed is nestled into an alcove. The composition faces the solarium, and a large mirror behind the headboard reflects the terrace gardens and sunlight. Shelves, cabinets, and a pull-out tray were all integrated into the alcove. We painted the walls a strié French gray-blue and selected a single French cotton print for the headboard, chaise, and curtains. The arrangement for the curtains was a bit tricky. I do not like long curtains on short windows. Among other things, they make a room look patchy. We installed cabinets beneath the small windows, giving them a base, and opted for festoons. The door to the solarium was not as challenging: it readily accepted one long pair of curtains.

Like the other rooms in the apartment, the entry foyer had a set of unique demands. Consisting of a series of doors—to the master suite, powder room, closets, and kitchen—that did not and could not align, the space was neither interesting nor distinctive. But what could not be done architecturally could be achieved through imagination and paint. Our solution was trompe l'oeil paneling reminiscent of that used in eighteenth-century French manor houses. The doors now seem less obtrusive, and the faux-bois Parisian grayed oak has a "thirsty" quality to it and an Old World feel.

What really strikes me about this project is that it evolved from my recollections of rooms I had worked on with Mrs. Parish as well as my clients' memories of the places they had lived in and visited in Europe. The design represents our accumulated visual memories, almost as if we had sat down with our scrapbooks. Inspiration doesn't always arrive right away. The direction we chose was one that found its home over time.

opposite, ENTRY

PREWAR TOWNHOUSE,
POSTWAR ART

In decorating, the proverbial question is often, where do you start? In the case of this Upper East Side townhouse, it was with a selection of mantelpieces, which set the tone for each room. Equally important was the clients' collection of art, which was to focus on postwar works.

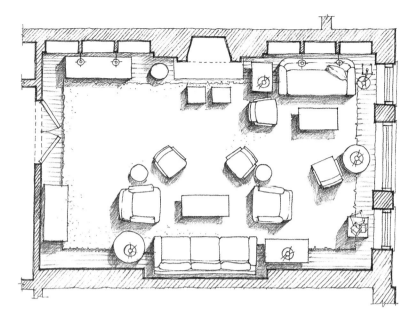

In the living room, a nineteenth-century green marble mantel is centered in the room. Typically a symmetrically placed mantel is flanked by a pair of sofas. I wanted to do the unanticipated and opted instead for multiple seating areas, putting one at the very end to draw visitors into the room. In Paris we found four 1950s Jules Leleu fauteuils, which act as a nice foil for the Empire stools and the Directoire side tables, not to mention the more relaxed upholstered sofa. The original oak paneling was beyond restoration; we installed new paneling that would mimic oak that had been warmed by years of exposure and waxing. As a rule wood-finish paneling can soak up light; painstaking care was required to get the soft, satiny finish just right. I needed to take full advantage of the daylight admitted by the fourteen-foot-high windows so we used unlined silk taffeta for the drapes. I also wanted the windows to be a pivotal moment so I established a hierarchy: the middle one favors a center draw and the side ones have asymmetrical swags, creating a unified window from three individual apertures.

Once we had established the furniture layout, paneling, and window treatments, it was time to install the new art collection. I remember the day when the wife called me over to see Hans Hofmann's *Don Quixote*, from 1963, hung above the sofa. The graphic quality of the painting completely transformed the room. It had been a little quiet: suddenly there was motion. Flanking are David Smith *Nudes* from 1964. A Jedd Novatt bronze sculpture is perched in the corner.

In general I am not a fan of the term "eclectic mix," which too often leads to sloppy improvisation. The dining room, however, is a perfect case for making an exception. The mantel is eighteenth-century Italian, the table Anglo-Indian, the chairs French Empire, the chandelier twentieth-century Venetian, the lamps French Art Deco, the mirrors American, the rug a nineteenth-century Oushak, and the console English Regency. As a rule, none of these things should go together, but this particular selection becomes a subtle argument for mixing different places and periods. If only the world got along as well as this furniture does. Francesco Clemente's *New York After Hours* hangs above the console, and a Richard Serra oil-stick drawing above the mantel. An Andy Warhol *Shadow* silkscreen marries the two.

The tonal palettes in the living and dining rooms are neutral, as requested by the clients, but in the library color is more prominent. This room took its cues from the Regency specimen marble mantelpiece. Its regal quality inspired bird's-eye maple paneling, Egyptian Revival–style bookcases in burled wood, and claret red upholstery. Computers, a sound system, and a television screen are hidden away behind doors with handmade silver- and bronze-tone mirrors. A Richard Diebenkorn hangs above the mantel, and a Robert Rauschenberg above the sofa.

Because the library functions as the husband's office, his bathroom is adjacent. It was inspired by the great Old World hotels like Claridge's in London and the Ritz in Paris. The strongly veined marble exudes masculinity; nickel trim offsets it with a modern crispness.

I like to think that there is a correctness to these rooms. They are not trendy or fashionable, making it hard to tell exactly when they were decorated. I wanted to recall the formality and architectural stature of the interiors described in the novels of Edith Wharton (and also in her volume with Ogden Codman, *The Decoration of Houses*). On the other hand, my client wouldn't be descending the stairs in a long, bustled skirt. The challenge was to apply a sense of decorum suitable for a young family in the throes of collecting a bold collection of modern and contemporary art.

EAST HAMPTON
SHINGLE-STYLE
COMFORT

I worked on this classic, 1920s Shingle-style house in East Hampton for the clients of the East Side townhouse. We set out to design a family-oriented country place that welcomed shoes-off, T-shirt living. Solid furniture that evinces the handwork of its creator, a distinct use of fresh and summery colors, bold art mixed with ceramics and pottery: these were the key ingredients in setting off the classic American architecture. The antiques and midcentury furniture we acquired represent the last gasp of the Paris flea market. Today, the world of point-and-click has made anything available from anywhere. When we chose the pieces for these rooms, it was still possible to make an unexpected discovery. We sorted through the jumble sale of Les Puces with a discerning viewpoint to make our treasures part of a cohesive, far-away design scheme.

previous spread and above, LIVING ROOM

PLAN, LIVING ROOM

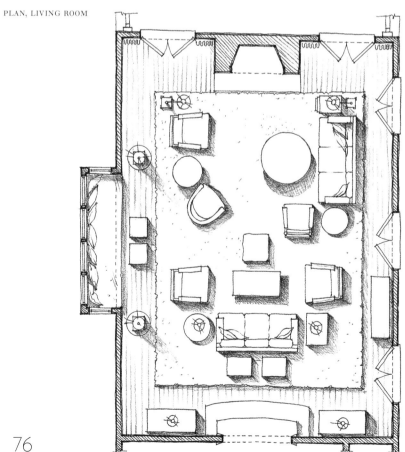

I find a room more interesting when it can't be taken in with just one glance. Here, the living room is a carefully composed medley of multiple seating areas, important antiques in varying shapes and heights with color splashed on pillows. Though smaller in scale, a leather chair by Jacques Adnet stands up to oak-framed armchairs by Jean Royère and a Maxime Old end table. A masculine Suzanne Guiguichon cabinet balances the whimsical pattern on the pillows. An antique Italian sunflower mirror hangs above the plaster fireplace, which is original to the house. All of the elements in the room correspond and relate, but they do not repeat.

We opted for mostly midcentury oak furniture in the dining room because the tone of the wood and the modern aesthetic juxtapose beautifully with the traditional architecture. The 1940s French table, which can be extended, is topped with a collection of ceramic jugs. The 1950s Maxime Old chairs are still upholstered in their original spruce-green leather. The craftsmanship of the furniture is its most notable feature.

DINING ROOM

A David Salle painting dominates the oak-paneled library, which doubles as a family room. The children watch television and play board games, and the parents review art and auction catalogs, so naturally the room gets great use and called for durable design. A Chanel-style sofa upholstered in linen runs the length of the windowed wall. An indestructible 1940s French Roger Capron coffee table made of glazed terra-cotta tile sits low to the ground on top of a leather and linen rug.

The ocean is visible from the corner master bedroom; to pay homage we painted the walls a creamy white. Offsetting the neutral walls are carefully placed punches of blue, such as the 1950s porcelain lamp by Paul Hanson and pale aqua cotton-stripe curtains. The curved midcentury oak desk is placed at an angle to offer views from both windows and soften the square corner. Our exuberant headboard design relates to the whimsical shapes of the Hans Wegner Mama Bear and Papa Bear chairs in the window bay. My clients acquired the ceramic lamp on the desk at a local antiques shop; we all responded to its tactile quality. The textile above the fireplace by contemporary artist Laura Owens adds another decisive punch of color to the otherwise soft palette of the room.

The newly built pool house accommodates lunches for family and friends. Almost everything in it came from the Paris flea market, including the 1940s beach scene hanging on the kitchen wall and the wooden globe lanterns. Twenty-two-foot ceilings are grounded by a set of 1940s oak-frame chairs, two coffee tables, and a Jean-Michel Frank–style sofa. The 1950s barstools are a reissued design by Jean Prouvé; the two British-colonial brass extension lights are early twentieth century, from India. We used sky-blue washed linen on the upholstery and blue stone for the floors.

This modernist seaside home is an ideal extension of the more formal and traditional life these clients have in the city. To move something forward, you don't have to push it over the edge. We gently nudged a classic house toward a relaxed and fresh aesthetic with modern furniture shapes, playful color palettes, and casual, carefree materials. The family's state of mind changes the minute they arrive for the weekend and kick their shoes off at the front door.

AT HOME
IN A CLUBHOUSE

The Alotian Golf Club, located on the outskirts of Little Rock, Arkansas, though newly built, suggests a classic Southern nineteenth-century manor house, one that has been restored and expanded over time and is furnished with pieces that have been passed down through generations. I wanted Alotian and its surrounding cottages (there are four) to feel residential and developed a series of rooms that are proper and gracious without being buttoned up. High-quality English and American antiques, top-shelf reproductions, and custom upholstery all contribute to the nuanced atmosphere.

People always worry about mixing antiques with reproductions. The key is to respect the scale of the antiques. Reproductions are often scaled up for modern comfort, and they can overpower older pieces. Finish is another thing to watch for. Don't put a wood-finish reproduction beside a wood-finish antique; the reproduction always suffers in comparison. A painted-finish reproduction next to a wood-finish antique would be the better choice.

We put these theories into practice in the main living room. We began by establishing two almost, but not quite, mirror-image furniture arrangements separated by an oversized skirted table surrounded by a set of four reproduction chairs. "Almost" is the operative word. Two antique eleven-foot-tall Macassar ebony armoires line one side of the room, while a low Continental chest of drawers is placed on the opposite side. In place of the typical antique rug, we chose a bold honeycomb design in stronger shades of the browns and blues used elsewhere in the room. We designed low, creamy white parchment tables and mixed them in with antique side tables and generously proportioned upholstery.

PLAN, PUBLIC ROOMS

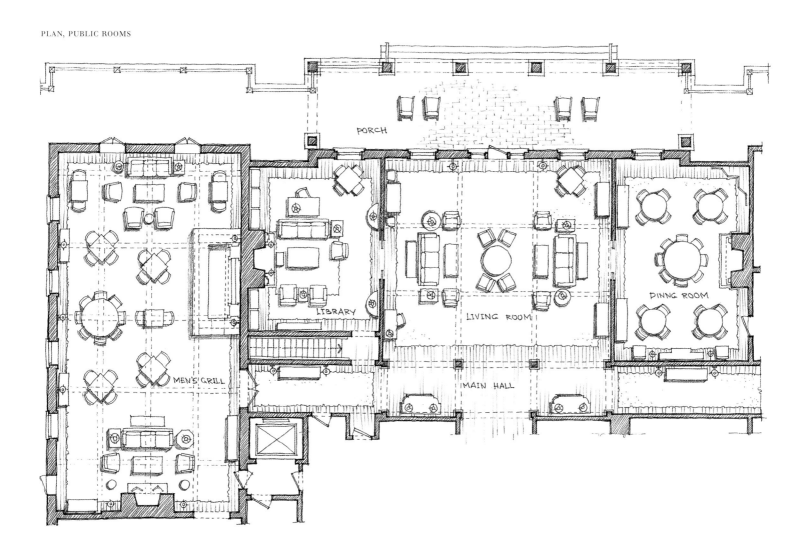

The living room curtains offer another important play on scale. The windows along the far wall stretch from floor to crown molding; the curtains needed to make an equally impressive statement, with detailing that could be seen from across the room. My answer lay in bright, graphic, looping wool-felt trim on a dark brown, wool-satin base cloth.

The finish of the new pine paneling in the library was an important contribution to our emulation of an old house. I had settled on the color of a worn, cherished baseball mitt, and it took us countless tries to get the degree of wax and depth of color right. Tufted leather chairs set a comfortable tone, especially alongside upholstery finished in a masculine paisley print. The room embodies the Old World sensibility we were seeking.

In two of the rooms I pasted fabric directly to the walls for a crisp look. Pasted-on fabric is never thought to be wallpaper; it still reads as fabric. In the dining room I used a cotton floral; the fabric is repeated for the curtains on the one window in the room with straight gingham curtains hanging behind. The scale of the room is large, which can often read as formal; combining the two fabrics keeps the room fresh. In the men's grill, I used burlap stenciled in a stylized tree of life pattern. Burlap alone would have been purely masculine, but the stenciled design brings a hint of femininity and decoration to the room. In fact, I'm often told I design masculine rooms that women are comfortable in, and this room speaks to that.

Twin screened porches at each end of the clubhouse are furnished with Aiken sofas, a version of the classic American porch sofa. (They were also a favorite of Albert Hadley's.) Here I scaled down the original design, which is really meant for napping, and developed a chair based on the same model. We mixed wicker with pieces like an iron twig mirror and called for lots of ferns and lanterns.

Even though our goal was to make Alotian feel like a wonderful old home in the South, we realized that it was ultimately a large clubhouse that needed to serve the needs and likes of its many members. We humanized the rooms and kept the mood young. Despite the high level of detail and carefully orchestrated play on scale, I find that Alotian has a certain simplicity, an almost humble, welcoming quality.

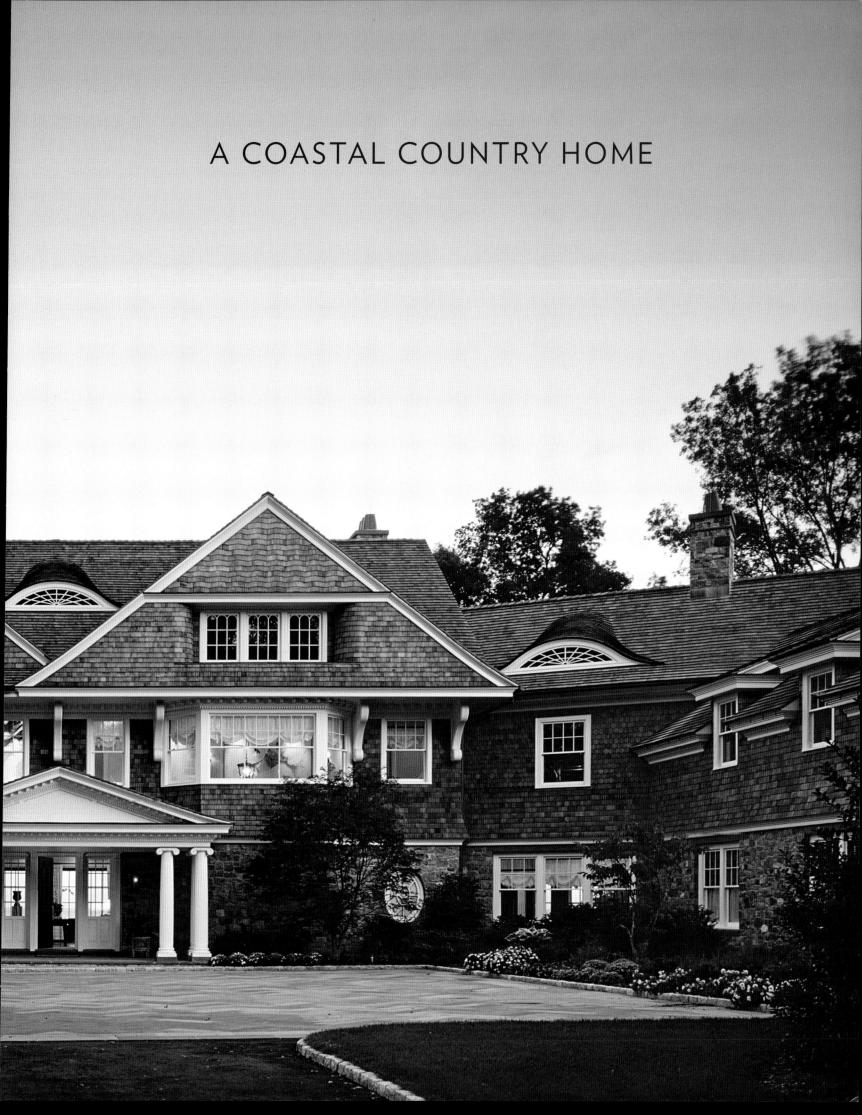

A COASTAL COUNTRY HOME

Sometimes, in an initial interview, clients give an idealized impression of themselves. Then you end up designing a house for people who don't exist. The clients who purchased this five-plus-acre estate on the Connecticut coast of the Long Island Sound, however, knew exactly who they were and how they wanted to live. They had replaced the original structure with an 18,500-square-foot house. A house this size could easily be regarded as pretentious; these clients were adamant that theirs would not turn out this way. The wife requested traditionally inspired rooms that would communicate a sense of ease, grace, and informality—that would support a rich family and social life. The husband had only two requests: a firm budget and a comfortable sofa in the library.

FOYER AND LIVING AREA

Although the house was classically inspired, the main rooms have a non-traditional open floor plan. From the double-height paneled foyer, the entire central section of the house reveals itself to visitors. The living and dining areas share one large space with more than fifty feet of windows overlooking the water; we decided on a neutral palette that wouldn't compete with the stunning surroundings. At one end of the room, seating areas are focused around a fireplace with an Italian limestone mantel; at the other end, a round dining table sits gracefully in front of a matching fireplace. A rectangular refectory table with low benches divides the room. The wife is fond of Italian furniture so we mixed painted pieces from that country with eighteenth- and nineteenth-century English and French antiques. We searched for pieces with fluid lines to relate to the Italian furniture, and rustic examples were always prized. Anything gutsy that could hold its own in the big space won the day.

This central area leads into a large kitchen and family room. Off the kitchen is the warmest room in the house, an eighteen-square-foot sunroom that doubles as the breakfast room. Simultaneously casual and elegant, it extends to the back patio and overlooks a pool and the sound. The room has a heated slate floor topped with a no-fuss cotton dhurrie rug and electric sun shades. I upholstered the furniture in nubby linens in sunny yellows and sandy whites and added linen-print pillows to summon the abundant blues and greens outside.

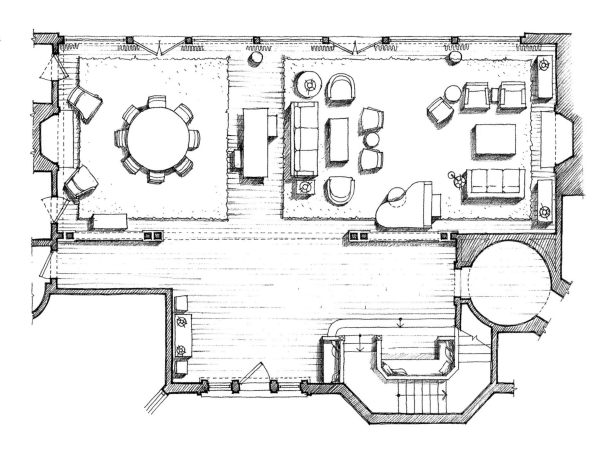

DINING AREA

LIBRARY

The family room is a study in scale. Big gestures bring the room into a comfortable dimension. We hung a large pewter inlaid mirror by Carlo Bugatti above the massive bluestone chimney mantel and chose an overscaled plaid for the curtains to bring the enormous windows into line. A reproduction wood chandelier also helps to fill the room and recalls the Italian furniture in the living area. Rather than mount the flat-screen television on the wall, where it would have looked minuscule, I designed a bronze easel for it to augment its presence.

As for the library, I started with the requested comfortable sofa and ended up designing the quintessential man-cave: mahogany paneling, a desk situated in the bay window where my client could enjoy views of his domain, bookshelves for an impressive collection of history and sports memorabilia. A television descends from the ceiling so that no sporting event is missed; a secret staircase concealed behind the bookcases leads to the master suite above.

The grisaille rose-patterned chintz in the master suite was inspired by my Parish-Hadley days. Bedrooms are a woman's domain, and though this room is abundantly feminine the gray keeps it from going too far in a direction that would make a man feel uncomfortable. Shell-pink wool-satin curtains soften the sea of gray. The cushions for the Italian Directoire chairs and sofa pillows introduce punches of cerise.

MASTER BEDROOM

The wife's study always makes me smile. The crescent-shaped, painted desk, which I found in London, is just right for my client. A pleated, scalloped valance was custom-designed for the curtains, which feature delicate Indian crewelwork.

My clients got what they asked for because they knew themselves and didn't hesitate to communicate that in a clear way. Each room is designed so that there is ample space for gathering with family and friends. Everyone says they want a house where the neighborhood kids come together; these clients ended up with that house: sports on the television, games on the lawn, and homemade pizza in the kitchen.

LOFTY COMFORT
IN TRIBECA

This Tribeca duplex loft was designed for a top Hollywood director and his family. Their main residence is in the rolling hills of Pennsylvania, and so we conceived of the loft as a reverse weekend house: it would feel urban but warm and enveloping at the same time. The director's specific instructions were to give it some carefully executed wow factors that would take the breath away.

LIVING ROOM

We began by gutting the space, a builder's spec loft chopped arbitrarily into rooms fitted with stock materials and standard hardware. Now the first floor accommodates the principal public areas, which are used for more formal entertaining, as well as two bedrooms that share a common sitting area. The upper floor is devoted to private spaces where the family can gather. My first wow-provoking decision was to replace the little black hole of a fireplace with a monumental construction inspired by Paul Dupré-Lafon, a 1940s French interior architect and Hermès product designer. The backlit monolith of contrasting honed and chiseled limestone with inlaid bronze floats against a wall of wenge paneling. It's a powerful moment when the elevator doors open.

MEDIA ROOM

Our second over-the-top gesture was replacing the boxy steps with an open staircase composed of cantilevered limestone blocks and a cast-bronze balustrade designed with artist Bill Sullivan. I wanted the balustrade to be very organic to balance the rectilinear quality of the rest of the space. Ironwork by early-twentieth-century French designer Edgar Brandt influences this naturalistic fantasy of twining branches, pinecones, and seedpods that seem to grow out of the steps. The stair divides the open lower floor into a large, more formally decorated living space on one side and a more relaxed area intended for meals and media on the other.

Another architectural element that needed tackling was the spindly wood columns the builder had installed. I replaced them with antique columns from a salvage company in the South. They had been stripped, so we decided to re-age them. The cast-iron patina we achieved resembles that of original columns found in other buildings in the neighborhood. The extra effort was worth it—they add an authenticity and a presence to the space.

opposite, STAIRCASE

As with most large lofts, the windows are only in the very front and the very back—the middle of the loft remains in darkness. We added a skylight above the stairwell to bring light into the center and concealed overhead pinpoint lighting behind frosted-glass ceiling panels.

When it came to the decorating, we were adamant that the space not feel like a downtown art gallery. We refused to consider stark walls, furniture on chrome legs, or glass-topped coffee tables, opting instead for a mix of midcentury-modern clarity and English-style comfort in luxe materials and finishes. Many of the furnishings we selected skewed toward tufted sofas, scrolled arms, and curved legs. The colors are a warm mix of creams, ambers, yellows, and browns, and the fabrics span from nubby linens and suede to silk velvet and taffeta.

MASTER BEDROOM

Although it was the wow factors that my director client empha-sized at the outset, I never lost sight of the fact that this loft was a city refuge for country dwellers. Many urbanites spend their weekends in pastoral settings. This family chooses instead to escape to the metropolis.

right, MASTER BATH
below, CHILDREN'S BEDROOM

MIDCENTURY MODERN
IN A CONNECTICUT
CLAPBOARD

When I first drove up to see this nineteenth-century clapboard farmhouse in Washington, Connecticut, I told the client, one of Hollywood's most successful producers, "The one thing I know for certain is that the house needs to be black." Staining it dark and painting the trim white would transform it from a clichéd Americana farmhouse to a modern New England barn. My client understood the intent right away, and this bold direction gave us confidence in one another.

We handled all elements of the design, from the front gates to the rock outcropping at the top of the garden. On the first floor Duane Dill of our architectural services department and I added a sunroom, breakfast room, and screened porch; upstairs we punched out the ceilings to create a master suite. We established gardens and replaced the 1970s pool house with an old barn that we bought, transported to the property, and reassembled.

LIVING ROOM

With the architectural footprint in place, we began the decorating process. My client amassed a significant collection of midcentury furniture and objects of art specifically for this house. A quick study, he became increasingly passionate about the period, and before long, we had built an assemblage that had the antiques world buzzing. The challenge was taking the collection and making it function for everyday life. There are no paintings or photographs in the house; my client was clear that the only things he wanted on the walls were mirrors and light fixtures by makers such as Diego Giacometti and Jean Royère.

left, BREAKFAST ROOM
below, LIVING ROOM

The living room is a veritable who's who of coveted midcentury designers. The coffee table is Paul Dupré-Lafon, the upholstered chairs are Jean-Michel Frank, the benches and wall sconces are Diego Giacometti, the standing lamp is Royère, and the mirrors and resin table are Line Vautrin. The original walls were rough plaster; we liked the textural quality, but they had a sad, flat effect that seemed to soak up light. To counter this, we upholstered almost all of the walls on the first floor in a nubby linen, which added warmth and modernity. In an effort to push the ceilings as far away from the floors as possible, we bleached and white-washed the rough-hewn beams and ebonized the floors.

Our goal was to make this house feel current while still respecting that it was built in the 1800s. We didn't want to hide our contemporary interventions: modern amenities are surely necessary for leading a comfortable country life. The state-of-the-art kitchen is stainless steel and white marble, and the bathrooms feature materials like oak, blue-gray limestone, and polished nickel. There is nothing "ye olde" in these spaces; they are polished and sophisticated with modern detailing.

My client is a bibliophile who has read and cataloged every book he owns. I lined the bookshelves in the library with oak to create the sense of a paneled reading room without producing an overpowering, claustrophobic effect. In front of the bookshelves a collection of Jean Besnard pottery sits on top of a pair of Jean-Michel Frank X-base tables. A pair of Jean Prouvé armchairs offer deceptively comfortable places for reading. To maximize space, I used a Eugene Printz desk as an end table for the sofa; a Marcel Coard chair and Line Vautrin lamp help it to double as a spot for letter writing and telephoning. I hung a Serge Roche mirror above the sofa to enlarge the room and finished with a gutsy Nakashima coffee table.

The dining room was intended for evening entertaining, so I opted to paint the rough plaster walls a blue-gray-green rather than continue the linen upholstery. The table is Nakashima and the surrounding chairs are by Kaare Klint. White plaster torchères by Serge Roche bring a needed contrast to the room, adding a sense of light even when they aren't illuminated. Country houses are expected to have filmy-white casement curtains. We decided to use pierced suede the color of a fawn; the weighty material holds up to the plaster walls but still filters light through to lend a warm ambience to the room.

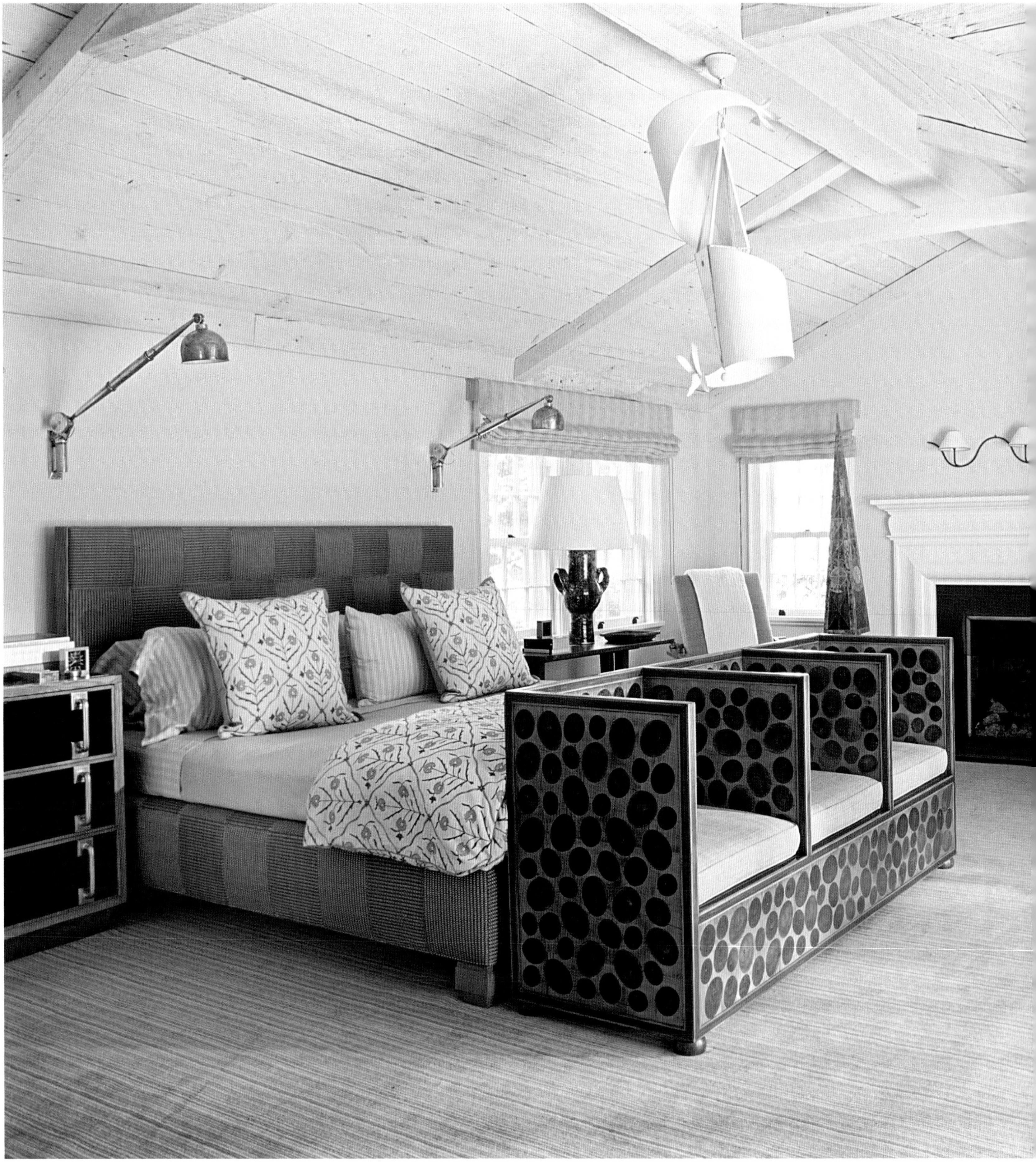

In the newly created master bedroom, we installed old timber on the ceiling and beams; drywall would have been a noticeable exception to the historical integrity of the rest of the house. No one has been able to attribute the quirky bench at the foot of the bed, but my client and I found its graphic quality irresistible. In lieu of a painting above the fireplace, a wave sconce by Royère has pride of place. Ruhlmann wall lamps above the bed provide ample light for nighttime reading.

The barn–turned–pool house is one of my all-time favorite spaces. It speaks volumes about seamlessly marrying masterful, modern architecture to one of our country's iconic forms. We removed the wall facing the gardens and mountains and replaced it with massive sheets of glass. A polished cement floor offsets modern black-steel and glass sliding doors. A stacked log box with stainless-steel banding encases the kitchen and bath in the center. Midcentury furniture fills the space and continues the modern aesthetic established in the house. The pair of hanging eighteenth-century lanterns is our nod to the period of the building.

This project resonates strongly because everyone involved was committed to a single objective. My client was willing to move beyond the concept of an 1880s clapboard house and explore a new direction. Our work together was as much about conviction as it was about execution. We both believed that honest materials and exceptionally sourced furniture, objects, and fixtures were paramount in realizing our vision. Nothing about this house is haphazard; every selection is considered.

URBAN CHIC
ON
PARK AVENUE

When my clients purchased this prewar Park Avenue apartment, it bore the scars of a dated, 1980s renovation. All of its original details had been stripped away, and the classic layout and delineation of rooms removed. The apartment had to work for both grown-up entertaining and kids' parties, and I wanted to create something that was beautiful yet comfortable, with no rooms or furniture that were off limits. I started by returning the space to an elegant, period-appropriate layout that would suit a young family with three children.

In many renovations, solutions evolve from obstacles that can't be changed. In this apartment, structural steel beams ran between the foyer and the living room. An oval rotunda, now a defining factor in the apartment, was conceived to camouflage the beams. The Robert Adam–inspired rotunda also paved the way for reinstating traditional elements like door surrounds, baseboards, and case moldings. Within this architectural context we created refined, understated interiors marked by classic furniture with modern lines.

My clients have a decidedly contemporary design sensibility, and one of their edicts was that there be no gold—this conjured images of bad FFF (fancy French furniture). I turned my attention to metals like nickel, steel, and silver plate combined with predominantly neutral, tending toward cool, color palettes. I assembled a collection of midcentury antiques, contemporary furniture, and custom-designed pieces in interesting materials like Macassar ebony, lacquer, mahogany, and parchment. This repertoire, which also includes doors lacquered ebony and dark-stained floors, provides continuity throughout the apartment.

The living room has an asymmetrical layout so I decided on two seating groups. A sectional tucked into the far corner of the room draws people in in an unassuming way. It is upholstered in silk canvas, which blends refinement with durability—a favorite combination. An André Sornay side table, Jean Royère coffee table, and Jacques Adnet lamp complete the tableau. In the second seating area, opposite the fireplace, a painting by Donald Baechler hangs above the sofa. The wood chairs are Lucien Rollin. For the pale blue silk curtains I used a grommet heading, which is deliberately modern and informal but not out of place.

Because the dining room doubles as a library I inserted book-shelves lined in cerused oak to emulate the warmth of a wood-paneled reading area. My clients often entertain other families so I designed two identical white parchment tables. Sometimes adults sit at one and children at the other, but there's also the option of joining them to create one long table. I installed the same cerused oak on the walls and ceiling in the after-dinner anteroom off to the side; this small space feels like the inside of a humidor, an intimate retreat for relaxing with a cigar and wine.

In the kitchen we abandoned prewar design principles in an ode to contemporary family life: the open floor plan. The large space has a breakfast and sitting area, which also functions as a playroom. Sturdy spill-proof chocolate-brown cushions form seating above storage drawers for games and toys. The children's artwork is at home next to colorful prints.

144

above and left, KITCHEN/PLAYROOM

We positioned the master suite at the end of the bedroom corridor so my clients could visit their way down the hall, putting the children and the house to sleep before ending the day in a private zone. The room is completely void of color, and the bed is set into a niche for an added layer of solitude and retreat. The walls are textured Venetian stucco, waxed and polished. Fresh and timeless, the bedroom epitomizes our goal for the apartment as a whole: something that this young family will call home for years to come.

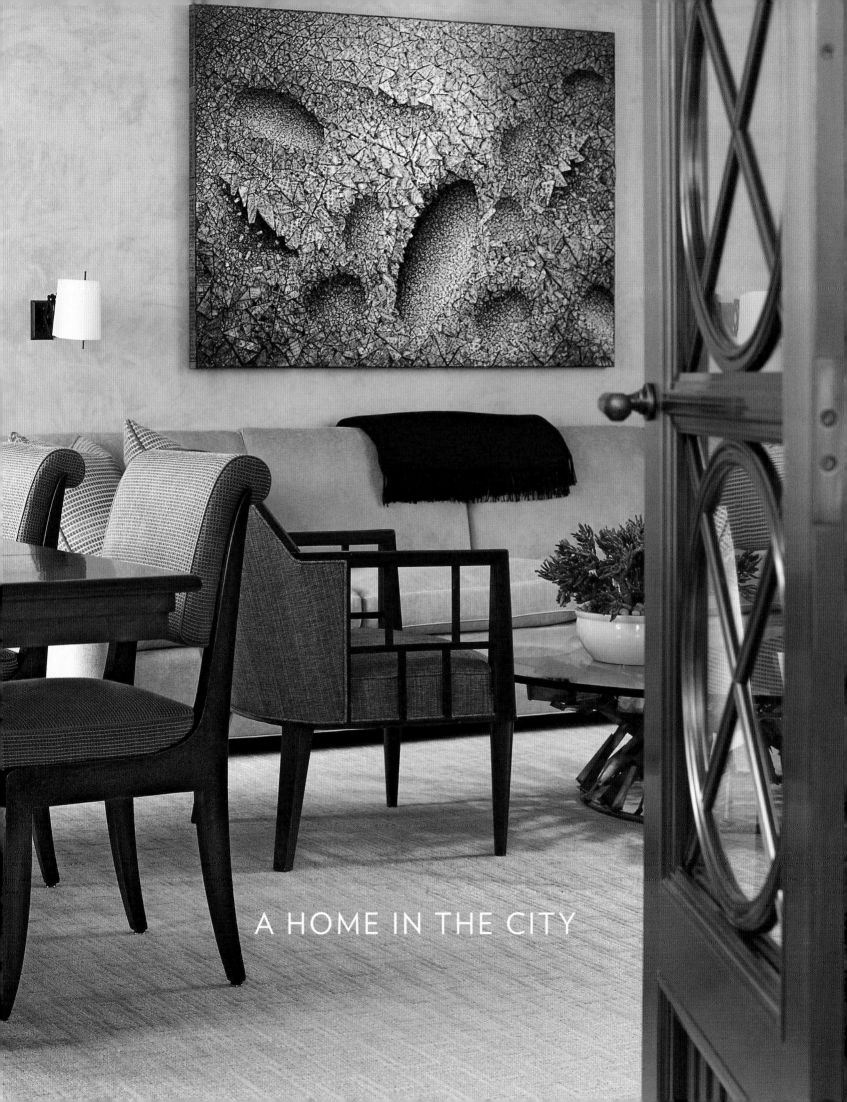

A HOME IN THE CITY

In every apartment or house there should be a cohesive thread that starts at the front door and continues to the back hall. It is the design equivalent of a trail of bread crumbs. In the case of this Upper East Side apartment, the first crumb was our decision to replace the original mahogany doors that appeared in almost every room. The doors made a statement, just not one that my clients liked. The parents of young children, they wanted to be able to close doors for privacy—but not at the expense of light.

ENTRY

I replaced the mahogany doors with a set of bronze-and-glass portals in a neoclassical circular grid pattern. I love the tactile quality of bronze; it's one of the few metals that exude warmth. Though not actually that tall, the doors add presence and weight, which makes the apartment seem bigger. There is a bespoke quality to them that keeps them from looking like something found in a bank. They also form an enfilade, opening the view from one room to the next, expanding the apartment's line of sight.

In the front hall, a limestone grid on the floor, the circular shapes of the door mullions, and a Danish glass chandelier speak to one another. I came upon the round center table in Paris, and I immediately knew it was right for the space. It was from an old ship and has a weighty steel base with a sphere in the center that recalls an ancient astrolabe.

152

POWDER ROOM

For the library, we wanted to avoid the typical dark mahogany. I based my wall treatment on square, cerused-oak panels designed by Jean-Michel Frank. But instead of a wood finish, I decided to paint the panels a high-gloss, creamy white and continued my design trail with a bronze inlay. Roger Thibier's set of gilded coffee tables echoes the square motif, while André Sornay's round side table accents the circular pattern of the doors.

The powder room off of the library is one of my favorites. Bronze reappears as an inlaid grid on the limestone floors and in the bronze-and-marble vanity. We added liquid wax to the brown paint to give added depth to the walls. Dark walls obscure boundaries, making small spaces feel larger.

People often ask me, "How do you feel about working with things we already have?" My answer is always "What do you have?" In this case, my clients had collected a number of important pieces that we wanted to incorporate. In the living room in particular, I wanted to enrich the midcentury French style they favored. Diego Giacometti's bronze-and-glass console is flanked by a pair of 1940s French chairs. A 1937 French mirror by Pierre Lardin hangs over the fireplace, which is faced in bronze. The vintage Maurice Jallot armchairs are covered in mushroom-colored velvet, and the coffee table is by René Prou.

FAMILY ROOM AND KITCHEN

The design trail takes a small detour in the kitchen and family room. A movable screen—translucent fabric sandwiched between glass above; wood below—can be arranged to connect or separate the rooms. The wife can open it when she is in the kitchen or close it for a more traditional arrangement of rooms. With a table by Eugene Printz, the family room doubles as the dining room.

In the master bedroom I played up the room's most important feature, the bed, with a bold brown-and-blue woven damask. The colors are masculine, but the fabric itself is feminine. A series of small drawings hanging above the bed forms a large rectangular composition. Grouped together, seemingly insignificant works become more powerful

Nineteen-forties France prevails in the young daughter's pink-and-brown bedroom. The oak slipper chairs and ribbon mirrors are from the period. Two 1960s Danish chests in bleached mahogany reside at either end of the bed. Walls upholstered in a pale cotton stripe on a cream ground keep the room from becoming too sweet.

When I initially saw this apartment, the space was dim and ponderous. I knew my challenge would be lifting it out of darkness. The doors became the catalyst for bringing light into the center of the space, and the bronze became a leitmotif that ran throughout. There's a youthfulness to this apartment, and yet there's a sense of permanence that emanates from an overriding visual connection between each space.

A GALLERY OF
ART AND LIFE

There is a quintessential New York story behind this enviable Park Avenue residence, located in a building where there are two apartments, or "lines," per floor. The couple and their three children were happily living in a gracious apartment in the A line yet found themselves yearning for just a little extra room. Serendipitously, the apartment in the B line became available, and the family soon found themselves with something quite a bit larger. Astute and knowledgeable, the couple asked us to combine two already large apartments in a way that would not seem cumbersome or overly grand.

CENTER ROTUNDA

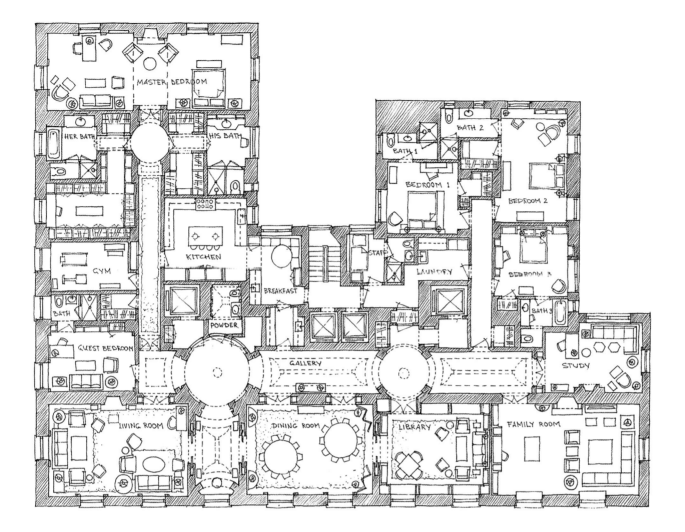

MASTER BEDROOM

HER BATH

HIS BATH

BATH 2

BATH 1

BEDROOM 1

BEDROOM 2

GYM

KITCHEN

STAFF

LAUNDRY

BEDROOM 3

BATH

BREAKFAST

BATH 3

POWDER

GALLERY

STUDY

GUEST BEDROOM

LIVING ROOM

DINING ROOM

LIBRARY

FAMILY ROOM

Our design solution: build one architecturally driven gallery that would span the width of the two combined spaces. As the main avenue for the two apartments, the hall needed to function in a variety of ways. I wanted to create intervals and points of movement, but by the same token I didn't want to interrupt the expansive sight line. We created a series of generous openings to the front rooms and introduced rotundas in areas that called for more than one doorway. The center rotunda, which connects to a windowed passage between the living room and dining room, brings light into the apartment and at the same time allows for a dramatic entry point. I have always been partial to lacquered doors with geometric motifs and am constantly working variations on the theme. These are perhaps the ultimate version: curved, mirrored (which required hand-molded glass), and overlaid with nickel fretwork.

opposite, GALLERY

Though the living room is opulent, there is still an element of restraint, a word that has guided my style for years. I pay as much respect to a newly commissioned piece from an emerging designer as to eighteenth- and nineteenth-century Russian antiques. French Directoire mingles with midcentury designers such as Jules Leleu and Jean-Michel Frank. This interplay gives the room life, allowing it to be luxe without feeling pretentious.

From the clients' formidable art collection, we chose an awe-inspiring group of paintings: two Cy Twomblys, two Warhols, a Richter, a Rothko, and a Picasso, which is casually placed on an easel atop a side table. Remarkably, the room doesn't feel like a museum. Instead, creamy whites, pearl grays, and a silver-leaf ceiling create a deep mixture of texture and tone and expand the boundaries of the richly layered space.

I find the best collaborations are with clients who have an open mind and an open spirit. I often learn as much from them as they learn from me. I recall the day the wife brought an image of a peacock-blue room to a meeting and asked me what I thought about it as a color for the dining room. At Parish-Hadley we had an entrance hall nearly that color, and I was immediately taken with her idea. I fine-tuned the concept by selecting an intense lacquer finish and a particularly rich hue. On the floor is a custom-made pony skin rug stitched in patches of gray. Works by Richard Prince and Richter hang on the walls.

The layout of the dining room is structured around the couple's constantly changing schedules. A traditional dining area with one long table wasn't for them. Instead, we designed two round tables and a set of tufted leather chairs. Since a central fixture would not have complemented this arrangement, I suggested we treat the lighting as another work of art. We brought in the artist Sharon Louden, who works in glass and fiber optics, and she designed a remarkable ceiling of twinkling stalactites. In place of traditional crown molding, the walls curve directly into the light-filled ceiling.

The mahogany library is stained the richest possible brown and French-polished to the highest possible sheen. The doors to the concealed bar are adorned with hand-woven leather panel insets and nickel trim. The coffered ceiling plays two key roles: it conceals a few ill-placed beams, and it gives the room weight and dimension. I like it when one motif speaks to another, so I designed the wool-and-silk rug in a Greek key pattern that relates to the ceiling. A sofa upholstered in linen with bronze nailhead trim tucks into the niche between bookcases, and a Fernand Léger painting hangs above. Guests often retire to this room for after-dinner drinks.

The family room occupies the corner opposite the living room and is exactly the same size. Decorated in taxi-cab yellow and charcoal gray, it offers a relaxed atmosphere for television viewing, computer activity, homework, and board games. Zebra-skin rugs and beanbag chairs covered in Mongolian lamb add fun and whimsy to a room most often occupied by younger members of the family.

FAMILY ROOM

HER OFFICE

The wife's office—command central in this household—is strategically located between the family room and the children's bedrooms. With walls swathed in hand-painted silk, an homage to history's great lady decorators, it is a deliberate step back from the robustness found elsewhere in the apartment. The room is comfortably furnished for both reading and desk work, with a Robsjohn-Gibbings end table connecting an intimate seating area and a parchment-covered desk with a chalky white French Provincial stool covered in tiger-silk velvet. This room is timeless: it could have been decorated in 1930 or today.

New York kitchens are typically in the back of the apartment, which means that they are almost always dark. To counter this, we designed a space that would appear to be filled with light. Among the reflective materials are white glass, polished stainless steel, lacquer, and an illuminated hood above the stove. Thinly veined white marble is used on the counters, and the backsplash and stainless-steel cabinets are faced in barely translucent milk glass. The floor is seamless terrazzo. A wire-mesh frieze incorporated into the molding integrates the air system. In the breakfast room, a clear Lucite and brushed stainless-steel table allows an ostrich-skin-imprinted vinyl banquette to breathe beneath a Murakami painting.

We have done our fair share of glamorous powder rooms, but the apartment's main one is particularly striking. Attention to finish and material artfully comes into play. Hand-made mirrored panels create an inset for the Portoro marble vanity with polished nickel hardware and Fontana Arte mirror hanging above. The walls are waxed graphite; the only source of color comes from a Lichtenstein painting.

POWDER ROOM

My clients' private area starts with a rotunda that offers passage to three places. Her bathroom is on the left, his is on the right, and the master suite, newly enlarged, is straight ahead. In the center of the bedroom suite are a fireplace, a pair of 1950s Swedish chairs, and a Fontana Arte glass table. To one side is the sleeping area. I like beds that look like furniture; this one has a satinwood frame and a headboard upholstered in a very pale blue-green silk. A sitting area with a Swedish desk and a Sugimoto photo anchors the other side. The wall upholstery and curtains were inspired by a Renzo Mongiardino room. We created a pattern on the walls by joining lengths of a simple wool satin and a printed linen damask. The curtains are made of the same two fabrics: the wool satin panels have damask borders.

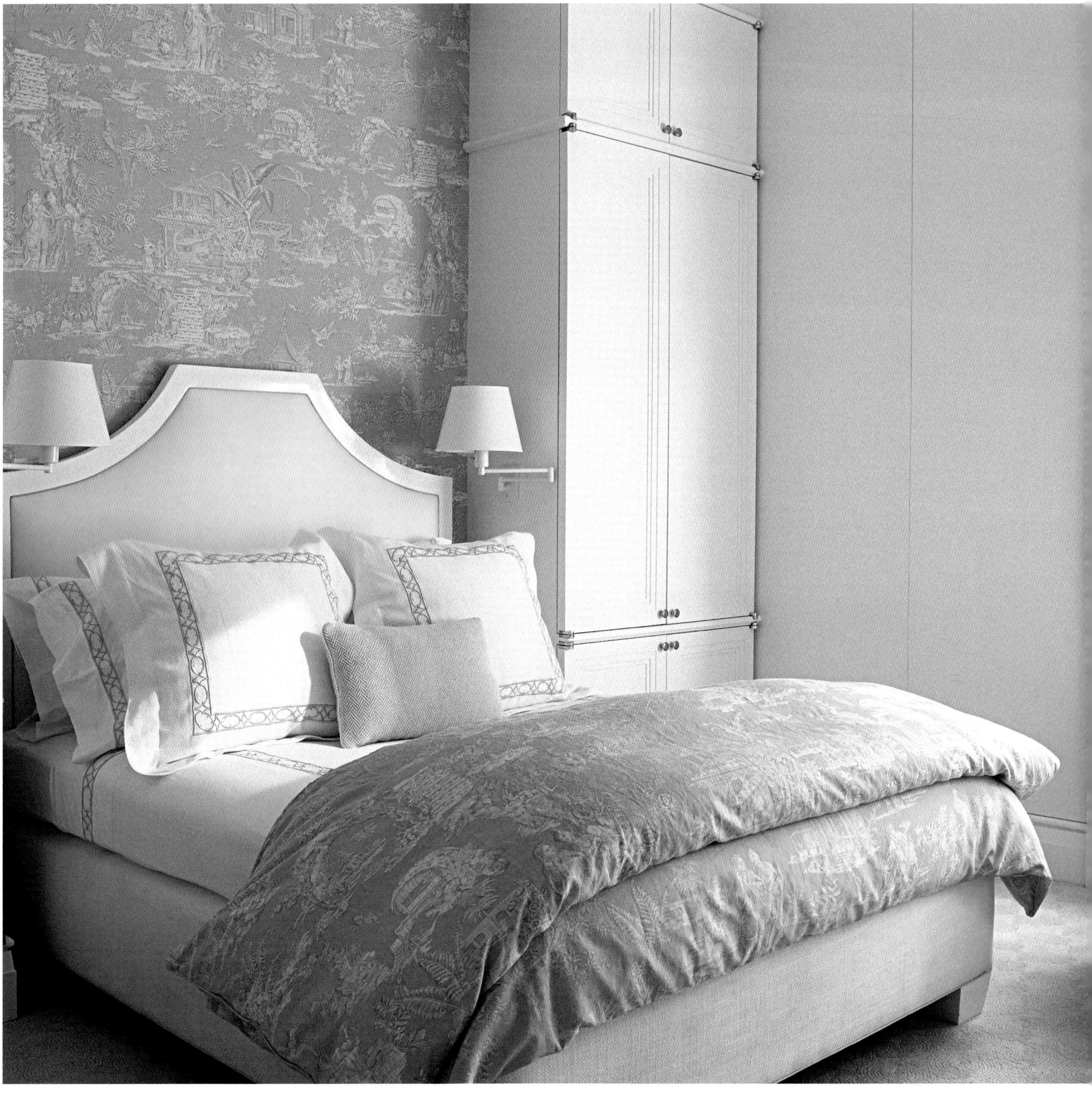

SON'S BEDROOM

Real estate notwithstanding, this apartment was generated by my clients' uncompromising commitment to interweaving highly detailed architectural design, complex decorating motifs, an important art collection—and an active family life. The sophisticated and luxurious interiors don't seem ostentatious because the design doesn't take precedence over daily pursuits. Stepping over a sleeping bulldog at the threshold to any apartment, no matter how grand, makes it feel like home.

FIFTH AVENUE
TREETOP DUPLEX

The first time my clients took me to see this Fifth Avenue duplex, it resembled a nice house in Connecticut, with walls covered in pine paneling, a traditional wood staircase, and Early American motifs. The rooms provided plenty of room for a large family, and the spectacular view took in the reservoir and trees of Central Park, but the character of the interiors did not suit my clients at all.

Like a couturier carrying around an antique textile, I have kept an image of a staircase from a London townhouse circa 1920 in my inspiration file for years. The stair hall provided not only the chance to reinterpret it—finally—but the opportunity to create a dramatic and ethereal space, a moment both high-glamour and modern. The area now functions as a nucleus of light around which key rooms orbit. The staircase is transparent and light but gutsy at the same time. The treads are floating limestone slabs, and the curved handrail is bronze. We designed white paneling for the walls and installed white limestone on the floors as well. The center table is made of steel and glass, and the lithographs are by Damien Hirst. A 1960s Italian chandelier unites the two floors. No matter how often I visit, this space takes my breath away.

The first level of the duplex comprises a kitchen and dining room on one side of the stair hall, a library/study on the other, and a large family area and guest room that runs the length of the apartment. We expanded the library to accommodate an office, which can be closed off with concealed doors. Walls, shelves, and storage cabinets are paneled in cerused oak. Wall-to-wall carpet connects the two spaces; a geometric, abundantly thick area rug defines the seating area. I chose corduroy the color of green moss for the sofa and mixed it with stone-colored suede and a nubby linen on the upholstered chairs.

In decorating, most people associate texture only with fabric; in fact, all materials have texture. Our design for the dining room wall paneling called for center panels finished in textured Venetian stucco; the disposition of the materials adds extra dimension. The paneling obscured the fact that the room wasn't completely symmetrical; it also concealed built-in storage cabinets. The table and chairs are contemporary designs, and the painting above the fireplace is Dubuffet.

The powder room is likewise an interesting mix of materials and textures. I wanted a deliberately icy and pristine feel, so I sheathed the space in glass panels reverse-painted in sea-foam green with specks of gold. A rather severe 1940s French mirror, composed of shards of glass, is an ideal foil to the sleek walls.

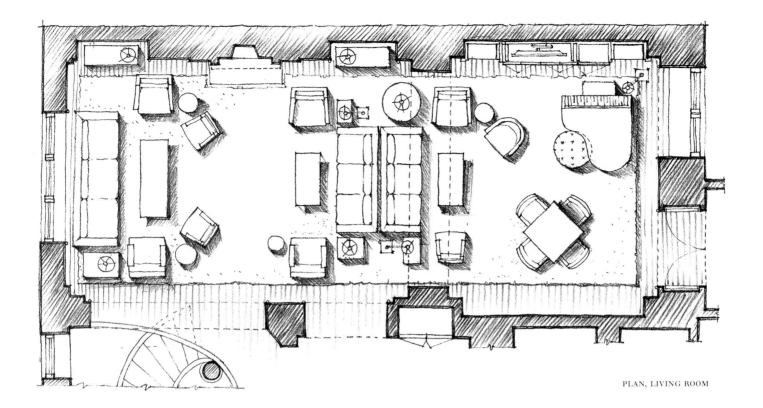

On the upper level are the living room and the family's private areas. Painted the color of morning fog, the elongated, asymmetrical living room takes on a loftlike quality. I had used paneling to solve the asymmetry of the dining room below; here I needed a new solution for rationalizing alignment. The answer became apparent in the two largest surfaces in the room: the floor and the ceiling. Neoclassical architect Robert Adam designed rooms in which the rug relates to the ceiling. I wanted to employ this strategy in a modern way and, with Duane Dill, head of our architectural services department, settled on a coffered ceiling and a geometrically patterned rug of our design with a slight play of depth.

Three principal seating areas anchor the space: one engages the view from the front windows, the second faces the fireplace, and the third addresses the game table and piano at the far end of the room. The curtains are made of pale gray silk with a border of raffia embroidery. The geometric motif references the ceiling and rug; all of a sudden plain curtains are no longer plain. We reproduced the mantel, composed of white and Bardiglio marble, from a nineteenth-century design. A mid-twentieth-century Italian mirror hangs above it. A pair of fruitwood Directoire chairs flanks the windowed seating area, and two French Directoire cabinets take ownership of the mirrored alcoves.

LIVING ROOM

One of the unspoken benefits of being a designer, especially in New York, is the prospect of looking into different spaces—large or small, elegantly proportioned or awkward—with different aesthetics—contemporary or traditional, casual or stuffy. Here we had a space that was enviable but somewhat suburban in feeling, and what my clients wanted was an alluring home evocative of their modern and urbane sensibility. The transformation delivers the drama and amplifies the sensation of floating above Central Park.

ISLAND VILLA

Hummingbird House on the island of Mustique was a long time in the making. The clients live in London, the architect lives in Venice, I am based in New York, and the house was to be built in the Grenadines. The project would be a labor of love—or possibly the end of our many years of friendly collaboration. But the complicated scenario ended up working to our benefit.

The couple envisioned a modern house but wanted to avoid austere, institutional clichés. What we achieved is an updated version of a classic island villa. The exterior is rough-hewn limestone set in elongated, horizontal bricks. The interior hinges on a central open-air great room with a spacious pavilion at each of its corners. Two smaller loggias anchor the infinity pool, one for dining and one for lounging. Our interiors, suitable for the rigors and traditions of tropical life, reinforce the symmetrical organization of the residence.

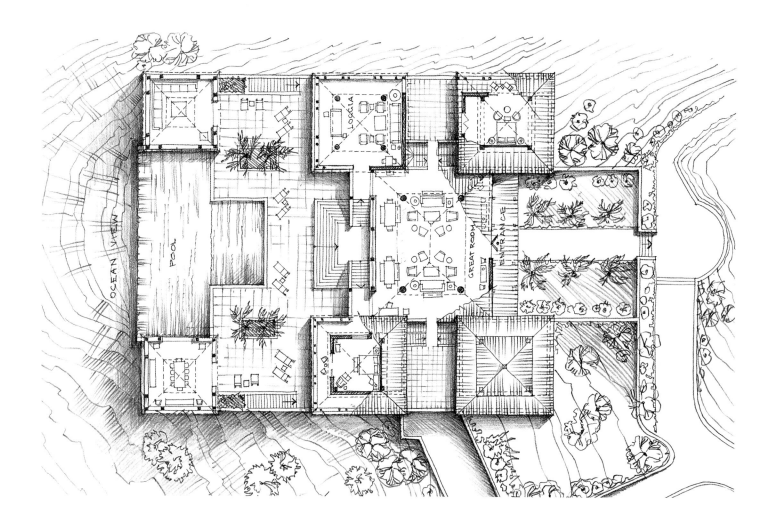

In the central living space, we wanted to combine the elegance and refinement of a Japanese tea house with the sturdiness of midcentury modern furniture. Four large posts support a twenty-foot-high roof; surrounding clerestory windows provide light and ventilation. Honed limestone is used for the interior walls, and the floors are polished mahogany with a limestone grid that connects the columns and helps delineate seating areas. Like the house, the furniture plan is symmetrical and accommodates an endless flow of guests.

We designed and produced every piece of furniture in the house, maintaining a strict point of view and carefully controlling scale, shape, materials, and layout. Getting the furniture just right had to take into account many factors. The tropical climate and open-air rooms limited our palette of materials. Teak, well suited for outdoor use, was the obvious choice, but we did not want our pieces to conjure pool furniture. We needed high-style and interesting finishes that could withstand the elements. The scale had to hold up to the large rooms. We covered everything in indoor-outdoor fabric: a wet bathing suit is as welcome as island finery.

right and below, GREAT ROOM BY DAY AND NIGHT

The master suite is a standout moment in sybaritic island living. The artisan who built the headboard and side shelves from a single piece of natural-cut timber is from a different island: Manhattan. Nevertheless, the composition appears to have been drawn from Mustique's indigenous landscape. Its rustic quality is balanced by a small settee at the foot of the bed, a place to pause and capture the dramatic view out to the Grenadines. An oversized marble tub floats in the center of the bath area, overlooking the ocean.

We tested the builder's patience with our proposal for the bedroom windows. We needed to provide relief from the heat and insects to ensure sound sleep, and so we created a three-paneled window system built into wall pockets. The first layer is a glazed window, the second a bug screen, and the third louvered shutters, which control light filtration. What is not required recedes into the wall. An enviable arrangement for ultimate comfort, this over-zealous, often-doubted, much-discussed solution was the first of its kind on the island.

What began as a project seemingly destined for failure resulted in one of Mustique's most coveted houses. The distance between the participants obliged us to collaborate closely. The architecture informed the interiors and vice versa. The sophisticated and cosmopolitan tastes of our clients required a design that is original and contemporary and that suits its location as well. The climate dictated certain parameters and solutions. The house is successful because it is the sum of its meticulously crafted parts. Taking away even one piece of the puzzle would have compromised the results of our labors.

POLISHED COMFORT IN
PALM BEACH

What strikes me most about the interiors of this classic Mediterranean-style house in Palm Beach is how closely they resemble the people who live there. I envisioned rooms that would be appropriate for a tall, strikingly beautiful blond woman and her confident, charismatic husband. The couple entertains often, and the husband stressed that they wanted a big little house. They asked for classic layouts and graciously sized but not sprawling formal rooms. The interiors, correct but not buttoned-up, have an enveloping intimacy and combine formality with youthfulness, not always the easiest blend.

LIVING ROOM

The formal layout of the living room accommodates two seating areas, a grand piano, and a game table. Occasional waves of pattern and the coffered, pickled-cypress ceiling keep the field of creamy whites and subdued golds from becoming static. Splashes of intense color from the contemporary art and punches of black from the piano and the Richard Serra oil-stick painting above the mantel energize and reinforce the youthful milieu of the space. The furniture ranges from a set of Biedermeier chairs around the game table to a bronze side table by contemporary furniture maker Ingrid Donat. The parchment chest is 1940s Continental.

The coffered cypress ceiling continues in the dining room but in a radial, star-shaped pattern. In decorating one recurring question is whether to play to or against type. Here I wanted to marry classical pieces with surprising choices. Louis XVI–style chairs surround a neoclassical table we designed. A 1940s Italian chandelier lends a modern air to the setting. The walls are treated in very subtle stripes of tone-on-tone Venetian stucco, adding nuance and depth to the intimately scaled room. The curtains are assembled of two layers of bronze organza; the horizontal pleated detail is a dressmaker-like effect.

Cypress reappears in the library, this time as paneling stained and polished a warm cognac color. To enhance light from the arched windows I installed sheer linen casements banded in tobacco-brown cotton satin. The Art Deco Giò Ponti desk is a refreshing counterpoint to the traditional paneling. A pencil drawing by Andy Warhol hangs above the limestone mantel, and a rug made of woven raffia and suede accentuates the informal mood.

LIBRARY

During the milder months, my clients enjoy time outdoors. Since the house is intentionally not terribly large, we wanted to extend the living space into the garden. A loggia that looks out to soaring palm trees, pink bougainvillea climbing cream-colored stucco walls, and the shimmering pool expands the footprint of the house and is connected to the natural order and flow of the interiors. A dining table generous enough to seat twelve anchors the central portion of the loggia; at one end is a fireplace that often serves as a backdrop for pre-dinner drinks. Coffered cypress ceilings allude to those inside and make the space feel like a proper outdoor room rather than a porch.

The master bedroom suite is awash in sea-foam green and white and opens to a terrace overlooking the pool and gardens. I decided to avoid the bench so often seen at the foot of a bed and selected instead two generously sized upholstered chairs and an ottoman. My clients often host guests, and this arrangement turns the bedroom into a private retreat where they can read the morning papers, catch the news, and enjoy coffee before heading downstairs.

It is always a pleasure to think about my clients inhabiting the rooms we have worked so diligently to craft just for them. I imagine this couple barefoot and casual on a Sunday morning or dressed to the nines to receive friends for dinner. Whatever the pursuit of the day, their environment allows them to feel very much at home and thoroughly self-assured.

MASTER BEDROOM

THE DESIGNER
AT HOME

Over the years, the one question people have always asked is whether being my own client is the hardest role to play. My answer is yes and no. In each home I have designed for myself—a walk-up apartment, a glass box in the sky, or my current apartment, a prewar residence once inhabited by George Gershwin—I have been able to envision precisely how I wanted to live. But when I am designing for myself, I am doubly impatient. It has taught me to respect my clients for the patience and poise they have exhibited.

Mara Palmer helped me find my first New York City apartment, a 250-square-foot, fifth-floor walk-up with a marble-faced fireplace on Lexington Avenue. The year was 1976, and I followed the aesthetic of the times: white walls, silver mini-blinds on the windows (which overlooked an air shaft), and floors covered in gray industrial carpet. I decorated the space with a traditional pull-out sofa upholstered in cream-colored, gaufraged damask and a white-lacquered linen Karl Springer coffee table. The only antique in the space was a drop-front Biedermeier desk. I could not have been happier: I was working for Mara, I could pay my own bills, and I could walk home from Studio 54 at sunrise.

A friend of a friend led me to my next apartment, on Sixty-seventh Street between Fifth and Madison Avenues, which seemed like a pretty swell address. Though there were two bedrooms and one bath, the view was still of an air shaft. By this time I was working at Parish-Hadley and was inspired to go all-out with the decorating. I glazed the walls moss green—to camouflage the lack of light—and Albert Hadley "loaned" me a kidney-shaped sofa that I upholstered in chocolate brown silk. I still have it today. I paired it with the only family heirlooms I really liked: my grandmother's slipper chairs, which I covered in a chocolate brown and natural linen print. On the wall opposite the sofa, a long rectangular table with a brown felt skirt became my storage attic.

In the master bedroom, I covered the walls in a print I still use, an oak leaf pattern in a lattice design. The curtains were brown wool felt with thick cotton bullion fringe, also in brown. I didn't really need two bedrooms, so in the tiny second room I installed a wall of closets with mirrored door fronts and created a dressing room—the ultimate luxury.

I remember thinking that if I never lived in anything more elaborate, I had already done better than I ever thought I would. But I returned home late one night from a buying trip to Paris and London and found a broken elevator, burned-out hall lights, and a fallen bathroom ceiling. It was time to go.

opposite and below, EAST SIXTY-SEVENTH STREET, LIVING ROOM

Light starved as I was, when a broker took me to a 1,300-square-foot glass box in the sky at U.N. Plaza, I was instantly hooked. I had just left Parish-Hadley to open DKDA, and I set about drawing my plans as if for a vast estate. The brown sofa went to storage, and I gave full reign to the more contemporary, architecturally strict style I had been gravitating toward. I wanted the space to convey one cohesive statement: the idea of Cole Porter in the sky.

My most dramatic architectural addition was a shoulder-height wall in the living room that functioned as a kind of permanent screen. It defined the entryway on one side and anchored the sofa on the other, but without obstructing the skyline view. For the floors, I opted for the darkest finish possible, a strategy that lends an illusion of height to low ceilings. At night, the sleek ebony parquet melted into the dark void of the city. I replaced my old Biedermeier desk with mid-twentieth-century pieces, and in the decoration I pushed the envelope of understatement as far as I could. Everything was "almost gray" or "muted brown"; the upholstery was done in men's-wear-inspired fabrics.

U.N. PLAZA, LIVING ROOM

U.N. PLAZA, MASTER BEDROOM

In the bedroom, I created a square-paneled alcove based on the work of 1940s French designer Paul Dupré-Lafon. This design, which seems to allow the bed to tuck into the wall and accommodates a bedside table and a desk by T. H. Robsjohn-Gibbings, has become one of my favorite architectural treatments.

On the day I moved in, I sensed the apartment was too small; and I still remember the clarity with which I realized that the space felt cramped once I started entertaining. The writing was on the too-close walls, and I ended up staying just over a year.

For my next apartment I opted for the convenience of living near my office and near my clients—on East Sixtieth Street overlooking the East River. The apartment was a larger, more comfortable version of the direction I initiated at U.N. Plaza. I started by reconfiguring the space, expanding the sight lines to make the space feel larger. There were three and a half bathrooms, which seemed excessive for one man, so I removed the powder room to create a more generous square foyer. I lacquered the interior doors a shiny black—my biggest architectural gesture in a space that was mostly windows. And I put in a lot of details not normally found in new buildings: tall baseboards, crown moldings, custom-nickel hardware, and hefty bead molding around the windows.

above, EAST SIXTIETH STREET, LIVING ROOM

Much of the furniture I had collected for the U.N. Plaza apartment fit neatly into this space, but here each piece had a little more air around it. I found more 1940s French furniture for the living room—a coffee table by Jean Royère and brass-and-black-lacquer end tables by Maison Jansen. I made a concerted effort to add what I consider major color: pale blue silk on the seats of the nineteenth-century Danish mahogany chairs and pale blue wool on the pillows on the sofa. The same whispers of blue, gray, and linen white appear throughout the apartment: I wanted the colors to merge into the wall-to-wall sky at the deliberately curtainless windows.

EAST SIXTIETH STREET, STUDY

Growing up, I spent many winter holidays visiting my grandparents in Miami, and Southern Florida seemed like a natural choice when I began searching for a weekend home of my own. Palm Beach appealed to me because it is less hectic than Miami but still glamorous, warm, and within striking distance of Manhattan. I went on an exploratory mission with a realtor, but nothing piqued my interest. There was one building I had always admired: a 1960s six-story concrete-and-stucco apartment block on the ocean by Edward Durell Stone. In an almost tongue-in-cheek manner, I told the realtor that she would have to find me an oceanside space in that specific building. She did just that, and I bought the duplex apartment sight unseen, in estate condition.

226

For a structure built not terribly long ago, it needed a great deal of repair. I stripped it down to the concrete, resurfaced the walls, installed new floors, put in new bathrooms and a kitchen, and raised the ceiling an all-important two inches. I liked the original layout, with spaces for entertaining on the first floor and private rooms above. The straight-on view to the Atlantic Ocean remains the principal focus.

My decorating goal was to create an environment that would be warm and friendly when I opened the door and hassle-free when I closed it seventy-two hours later. I was determined to avoid Palm Beach decorating clichés—acid hues, palm-tree motifs, and seashells—opting instead for a strongly graphic, predominantly black-and-white color scheme. Punches of Florida-inspired yellow and coral are found only on the living room sofa pillows.

I have always had a predilection for streamlined twentieth-century furniture, and here I gravitated toward more rough-and-tumble examples from this period: a 1950s Italian lounge chair by Osvaldo Borsani, a limed-oak-and-bronze Art Deco, African-inspired cabinet, and a Belgian desk by Jules Wabbes that doubles as an end table. The moody, grades-of-black painting by Joe Andoe once hung in my U.N. Plaza apartment.

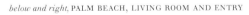

below and right, PALM BEACH, LIVING ROOM AND ENTRY

The work of Scandinavian icon Kaare Klint inspired my design for
the white-lacquer chairs in the dining room. I bought the drawing
by Chicago-based artist Jim Lutes at the "Works on Paper" show
at the Armory in New York several years ago. Recently his work
was featured in the Whitney Biennial. I never seem to get this sort
of thing right, but this time it was a lucky purchase.

PALM BEACH, MASTER BEDROOM

I've never had a colorful bedroom before, but I was so taken with a particular pale blue that I used it abundantly. The walls are a pale blue ground with white strié. I chopped the paper into large squares and created a basket-weave pattern, which produces a terrific texture on the walls. The linen curtains are the same watery blue, and the bed is covered in white leather squares that have been stitched together.

above and opposite, PREWAR APARTMENT, LIVING ROOM

In many ways my career—and my life—has been based on luck and timing. As a young man, I was invited to a swell lunch party in what seemed, to me, the most sophisticated New York environment imaginable: a full floor in a discreet prewar building that had once been home to George Gershwin. I had always aspired to the sort of gracious living I encountered that afternoon. Well, no sooner was I on the streets looking for a more architecturally interesting apartment than my trusted broker took me to see the very same apartment. I still found the elegantly proportioned living room, thirteen and a half feet high and flooded with light from floor-to-ceiling windows, irresistible, and I am now lucky enough to call this apartment home.

Yearning for a place to really hang my hat, I approached this as a permanent project. I was ready to return to interiors inspired by traditional design principles. Centered in front of the large-paned window in the living room is an Italian Directoire table flanked by a pair of wing chairs I based on twentieth-century Danish design. The work of Maison Jansen inspired the large black-lacquer cabinet, which houses a flat-screen television, at the other end of the room. Most important, there is an abundance of comfortable upholstery inviting friends to settle in.

Like a turtle, I tend to carry my shell with me. Many pieces from past residences have found a place of their own in this new environment: a pair of Danish neoclassical caned-back game chairs, a circular sculpture by Bruno Romeda, a bronze African-inspired bust on the fireplace that I carry around like a talisman. The newest members of this traveling band are an exuberant 1930s spiral chandelier, Swiss in origin, and a large oil painting by contemporary artist Garth Weiser that hangs above the sofa. To keep formality in check, I opted for a textured sisal rug.

In the dining room, I retained antique Chinese paneling (which I remembered from my years-ago visit); it is an enticing backdrop for a table by Raphael and an Art Deco light fixture, both of which I've owned for many years. A red-bordered mirror from the 1940s hangs above the fireplace, punctuating the more subtle gilded tones of the hand-carved paneling. The black cowhide rug on the floor is the velvet lining in this jewel box.

I needed to create an interesting ambience in the long hallway that provides the apartment's central access. I finished the vaulted center portion in a high-polish Venetian plaster; the soft glow of light on the domed surface sets it off so elegantly. Strongly reflective veined marble floors cast a watery reflection. The large slabs are installed in an alternating pattern to make the narrow space more visually exciting.

The master bedroom and the library/sitting room together function as a perfect suite of rooms. To enhance the effect of the classic raised panels in the sitting room, I upholstered the center panels in linen with nailheads in a grid motif. This treatment both provides a library-like nuance, which I felt was missing elsewhere in the apartment, and creates pattern from plain fabric. We upholstered the sofa in the same linen fabric and added mossy green cotton tape to create panels. There is no patterned fabric in the room, but it feels as though there is.

PREWAR APARTMENT, MASTER BEDROOM

At the end of the day—literally and figuratively—I am someone who finds comfort in neutrals. And by now, I know that the best approach to decorating is to be true to your instincts. My bedroom is my comfort zone, and I wanted to create a very Zen-like atmosphere, an unapologetic homage to no color. I used the same subtle stripe for the curtains and on the walls. The taupe carpet is a plush silk. Everything in the room speaks to being coddled in a restful, distraction-free environment.

Human beings are like water—we tend to fill the available space. But I'm a ferocious editor. Unlike many in my profession, I don't get fixated on possessions. People assume that decorators change their interiors like most people change their clothes. I prefer to keep the things I like with me. Mrs. Parish maintained that antiques offer a sense of time, place, and permanence. I agree; mine tell stories about the lives they lived and the life I am living, where I've been and, I hope, where I'm going.

PROJECT CREDITS

INTRODUCTION

CONYERS FARM
Architect: Alan Wanzenberg
Project Administrator: Kim Cruise

CALUMET FARM
Project Decorator: Vance Burke
Project Administrator: Kim Cruise

GARRICK STEPHENSON APARTMENT
Project Administrator: Kim Cruise

PARK AVENUE APARTMENT
Architect: Richard Rosen
Project Decorator: Brian del Toro
Project Administrator: Kim Cruise

SOUTHAMPTON HOUSE
Architect: William Schulz
Project Decorator: Luca Rensi
Project Administrator: Kim Cruise

KIPS BAY DECORATOR SHOW HOUSE
Project Administrator: Kim Cruise

AN EQUESTRIAN EDEN
Architect: Neil Turner Architects
Project Decorator: Luca Rensi
Project Administrator: Kim Cruise

FRENCH FLAIR IN NEW YORK
Architect: Ferguson & Shamamian
Project Decorator: Luca Rensi
Project Administrator: Kim Cruise

AMERICANS ABROAD RETURN
Project Decorator: Stewart Manger
Project Administrator: Megan Gavrity

PREWAR TOWNHOUSE, POSTWAR ART
Architect: Nasser Nakib
Project Decorator: Luca Rensi

EAST HAMPTON
SHINGLE-STYLE COMFORT
Architect: William Schulz
Project Decorator: Luca Rensi
Project Administrator: Megan Gavrity

AT HOME IN A CLUBHOUSE
Architect: Mark P. Finlay Architects
Project Decorator: Scott Sloat
Project Administrator: Megan Gavrity

A COASTAL COUNTRY HOME
Architect: Mark P. Finlay Architects
Project Decorator: Scott Sloat
Project Administrator: Kim Cruise

LOFTY COMFORT IN TRIBECA
Architectural Services: Duane Dill and Marina
Lanina/David Kleinberg Design Associates
Project Decorator: Sean Matijevich
Project Administrator: Megan Gavrity

MIDCENTURY MODERN
IN A CONNECTICUT CLAPBOARD
Architectural Services: Duane Dill,
Marina Lanina, and Felix Flit/David Kleinberg
Design Associates
Project Decorator: Sean Matijevich

URBAN CHIC ON PARK AVENUE
Architectural Services: Duane Dill,
Felix Flit, and Jair Gonzalez/David Kleinberg
Design Associates
Project Decorator: Nathan Andrew
Project Administrator: Megan Gavrity

A HOME IN THE CITY
Architectural Services: Duane Dill/
David Kleinberg Design Associates
Project Decorator: Sean Matijevich
Project Administrator: Megan Gavrity

A GALLERY OF ART AND LIFE
Architectural Services: Duane Dill, Grace Rais,
Marina Lanina, and Michael Wright/David
Kleinberg Design Associates
Project Decorator: Lance Scott
Project Administrator: Megan Gavrity

FIFTH AVENUE TREETOP DUPLEX
Architectural Services: Duane Dill
and Jair Jarek/David Kleinberg Design
Associates
Project Decorator: Scott Sloat
Project Administrator: Kim Cruise

ISLAND VILLA
Architect: Paolo Piva
Project Decorator: Nathan Andrew
Project Administrator: Kim Cruise

POLISHED COMFORT IN PALM BEACH
Architect: Smith Architectural Group
Project Decorator: Lance Scott
Project Administrator: Kim Cruise

ACKNOWLEDGMENTS

I would like to thank Albert Hadley for his generosity of spirit and support. Chesie Breen has been essential in every way to the creation of this book and has made all of it seem possible. Rusty Harper is the most multitalented assistant one could hope to have on a team. I am grateful to Andrea Monfried for her clarity and expertise, Rebecca McNamara for her thoroughness, Beverly Joel for her visual style, and Gianfranco Monacelli for making this book a reality.

I am grateful to everyone with whom I have collaborated over the many years. It is impossible to properly thank the talented and ever-patient architects and craftsmen. Duane Dill has worked alongside me these past twelve years, helping build what is seen in these pages. And thanks is overdue to the gifted team in my office. The most important thanks is reserved for my clients. I have been privileged to work for them, and to have been trusted with their homes and comfort.

— D.K.